THE LAU

IN THE ROOM

Alycia D. Jenkins

The Laughing Elephant in the Room © 2022 by Alycia D. Jenkins

ISBN-10: 1584410051
ISBN-13: 978-1584410058
Library of Congress Control Number: 2023907707

Renewing Your Mind Ink, a division of The Renewing Your Mind Foundation po box 1152, Pocono Summit, PA 18346

Visit our Web site at **www.PeaceInTheStormPublishing.com**

'... holy holy

jesus loves you
baby
& he forgives you
for getting shot

unless it happened
in math class
while you talked
to the boy you loved
but never told him
because you were scared
he wouldn't love you back
& in america
we'll give you
something
to be afraid of

or on your way
to recess
where it was your turn
for the swingset
& jesus

really wishes

your little legs

could run

faster[1]...' -brett a. maddux

---

[1] Blackbird 4pm. Brett A. Maddux Poem 'america, 12am' pages 8 lines 1-25.

"Behold, I stand at the door and knock: if any man hear my voice, and open the door, I will come I to him, and will sup with him, And he with me." **Revelation 3:20**[2]

Dedication to:

Dorval Jenkins aka Man-Man

May we all laugh!

Author's Note:

This book has taken me ten years to write, and I never thought it would ever become a book. It started out as a long poem in April 2012 when I studied abroad in Paris during my junior year of college. I saw an ad about the circus and the elephant was the face of this event. The elephant appeared, to me, as if it was laughing. I quickly took out my pen and my journal (that I just purchased in Paris) and wrote the title 'The Laughing Elephant' and quickly closed the moleskin. I wrote the first stanza that night and left it alone. When

---

[2] New King James Version Bible. Revelation 3:20.

I returned to the states, I began to write more to the poem and discovered that this work was going to be different from most poems that I've written in the past. I was given a message from my ancestors (albeit I'm paraphrasing) that was the following, "*We are laughing at you (whiteness) for not acknowledging the elephant in the room. We are laughing because the others in the room don't know our end game*". Once I received this message, my relationship with this project changed in three keyways: 1.) I lost the journal I wrote 'The Laughing Elephant In The Room' three times! 2.) Every. Single. Time. I wrote more to this story inexplicable things would occur. 3.) It seemed that I would tap into the spirit of my ancestors and the spirit of the elephants' cry whenever I'd read the words of this story out loud.

The reason for the title 'The Laughing Elephant in The Room', is speaking to the classic metaphor and expression that speaks to the elephant (racism/anti-blackness) being America's issue that "she" is not willing to fully confront. My plan with this story is to defy the notion of the elephant just existing; however, the elephant will ultimately destroy the room. Through the presence of the ancestors on the cover of this book, it has made me honor their existence within history and their connection to the story of them being the laughing elephants in the room. Also, in this book there is a *book of spells* that I form from my inner power which I share with my deceased brother through song. I use this power for the wellness of my people.

***

Lorraine Hansberry: When Lorraine Hansberry saw 'A Raisin in the Sun' gain success, she laughed with joy and cleverness within her sound. After I watched her documentary on Amazon Prime, I reflected upon the first time that I read her play 'A Raisin in the Sun'. I read the play in my junior year of high school. I participated in the school play as a student director which was a proud moment for me as a young Black female spoken word poet. Miss Hansberry taught me that I could actually write a play and/or a book. I always knew that I would write a book, but I never **believed** in my ability to author a book until I read her play.

James Baldwin: James Baldwin laughed in the

room when he said, "I am not your Negro..." for he knew that Black Americans are indeed American. He reclaimed the pride in building this country and knew that one day that pride will progress Black Americans forward. I read James Baldwin's masterpiece 'I Am Not Your Negro' in 2019. I began to realize that through James' words, my thoughts, beliefs, and voice are similar to his. I've been told when I was in college that I sounded like James Baldwin because of my deep belief in my people. As James Baldwin fought for Black Americans to be heard, I now fight for our voices to be felt and seen.

Harriet Tubman: Harriet laughed in the war room because she knew that freedom was near. She is the reason that I am pro-gun. Growing up, I remembered the picture that my grandmother had in her living room. This portrait of Harriet is of her in the woods with other Black people running toward freedom. Harriet has a gun in her hand. My Mississippi Grandma told me that this painting of Harriet is her favorite; and it is also my favorite.

Frederick Douglass: Frederick Douglass

laughed when he published the North Star. He knew that black voices were important and needed to be heard. Mr. Douglass walked with freedom in his footsteps and forced America to not only see the Negro people, but to believe and know that the Negro people are indeed human. He shook America to death. I am grateful for him shaking the core of this country and making it better.

Medgar Evers: Medgar Evens laughed with a booming voice, like that of thunder, as he fought for justice and civil rights. I was taught about this man through James Baldwin's, 'I Am Not Your Negro'. Medgar Evers reminds me of my father who has a big spirit yet little frame with a low and impactful voice.

Ida B. Wells-Barnett: Ida. B. Wells laughed a glorious laugh of truth that let folk know of the horrors of lynching. She laughed to keep from crying as she journeyed on her crusades for justice. The spirit of Ida came to me in March 2021 to give me a message. Her message was to tell the truth while carrying a 'shot gun' in my pocketbook; therefore, I carry my words on my tongue and share them with the world.

Martin Luther King Jr.: Martin Luther King laughed in the room once Black Americans gained the right to vote. White folk feared him when he spoke. His laugh was loud. Reverend King showed up in my dream and apologized for leading our people into a burning house. He had his arms open as if to hug me as if to thank me. I say that because of Mr. King, I am here with a clear vision to continue where he left off in fighting the last good fight for my people.

Malcom X: Malcom X laughed a sinister laugh in the room full of black faces when he said, "We declare our right on this earth to be a human being, to be respected as a human being, to be given the rights of a human being in this society, on this earth, in this day, which we intend to bring into existence by any means necessary[3]." He knew that it was time for black folk to rise. Mr. Malcom told me in the mirror that I will tell the truth by any means necessary. He laughed and told me to remember where I come from and not to forget about the power that I hold in my hands.

---

[3] Contributed by: *Blackpast* **www.blackpast.org** , 'Malcom X's Speech at the founding rally of the organization of Afro-American unity', October 15th 2007.

W. E. B. Dubois: W. E. B. Dubois laughed when the NAACP became a space for justice for the colored folk. He outsmarted the powers that be with his understanding of the Negro American's intellect. His honoring of the negro mind made his laughter roar across the heavens. Mr. Dubois is the reason why I'm anchored in the philosophical thought of my people. His writings have helped me honor those voices.

Toussaint Louverture: Toussaint Louverture laughed while he was imprisoned in France. His laugh rippled across the ocean to ensure a victory for Haiti's Independence. He knew freedom was near. He visited me in a dream the night that I moved into my first apartment. That night, I started to write more of this book and was filled with fire in my hand.

<u>Acknowledgments</u>

Firstly, I would like to thank God, myself, my ancestors, and my family and friends. I'd like to thank my family in the Poconos and in Chicago for believing in me to write this book. I'd like to thank my old Starbucks Crew from the land of the 860 in downtown Hartford, CT for *seeing* this poem become a book and enduring my relentless times of losing the journal. I would like to thank a fellow writer who helped me find the title to this book, I am forever grateful for her patience.

This book is for my ancestors who were deemed witches due to their dark skin because of the fact that they could heal. This book is for those who were deemed witches by virtue of being poets, songwriters, storytellers, and healers who need to always write what is right every day because you have to. This book is for my Mississippi, Chicago, Haitian, Alabama family. This book is for my grandmother, on my maternal side, who has passed and is always with me. I feel her presence evermore. I know she smiles as she guides me. I thank my grandmothers for teaching me how to utilize my #BlackGirlMagic. I appreciate and love these women in their essences. This book is for those who have very little voice and whose bodies have been massacred. This book is for me to use my voice to see myself as a valid being. This story is to teach the youth how to love themselves so that they can heal. No judgment. No hate. For there is no devil. For there is laughter, joy, power, and life. May the gods & ancestors be with me and my hands.

"Human am I
spirit am I
I have the infinite
Within my soul
All this I am
Human am I
Spirit am I
I have the infinite
Within my soul
All this I am."
-Margaux Hayes

This song is for The Laughing Elephants

In The Room

The Laughing Elephants that dare to be

loud

The Laughing Creatures that are drunk

with liquor in their trunks

The rock stars that dance at the foot of

the mountain

This rhyme is for the girls that wanted to

be their grandmothers and one day became

them with fire in their eyes and heavy metal in

her blood and tattoos on her face and angels

singing her grace and brick walls breaking and

red lipstick shining in the sun light

Yelling, 'Yea, that's my grandma!! The

coolest and the best in the WORLD!'

This nursery rhyme is for church goers

who are deep down 'laughing elephants'

themselves and they worship the devil they

seek and they cry with the dark cloud over the

pew as the pastor preach to the few

This lullaby is for The Laughing

Elephants getting the last laugh in the midst of

reparations

In the midst of keeping the elephant alive

In the midst of elephants crushing souls

In the midst of elephants breaking skulls

In the midst of The Laughing Elephants

smiling as black folk rise!!

This childhood ruined was for my past as

a seven-year-old who cooked with my grandma

who whispered to plants and locked eyes with

my Mississippi Haitian Alabama Chicago

side...

-The Laughing Elephant Pink

The Laughing Elephant

"The mist

Of flowers fragrance

Flow

Through the

Veins of the people

We sing

In harmony with

The petals

Of the

Wind

In red

Like roses

With

Thorns

Thick

With

Blood

And sorrow

In pink

Which represents

Realness

In blue

I hold my hands

And glisten with

The light of the sky

In yellow

The grace

Dances across

Our faces

When sleep is

No longer relevant

In purple

Like ice that never melts."

- The Laughing Elephant

The

Laughing

Elephant

lives

in

the

wake of the flames

and watches

the clouds

turn black

and smiles.

Have you heard The Laughing Elephant's laughter

trapped in your ear when you cannot dream?

It shakes you and wakes you to a brutal end.

It's trunks heavy with sound as the noise rings loud.

Listen to the laughter when your dreams cascaded

down your face.

Have you heard the laughter ringing in your ear?

Have you heard?

Be silent and feel the vibration, feel your body tremble

The Laughing Elephant waits for no-one

cares for no-one

Listen to the smile

of this Creature

Listen as it's laughter rings from the heavens

And

Sends

A ripple

Affect

Down your

Spine

Have you heard

The Laughing Elephant at night?

Watching you?

Holding your breath?

The Laughing Creature

is

lurking in our shadows

The Laughing Elephant

is

a Creature that lurks and waits for no-one

The Laughing Elephant

smirks

and plays with

your

mind

He dances in

circles

and

creates

magic

He's there in

your

ear

singing a tune

laughing

with little sorrow

in his

belly

he is the clown

of all

creatures

and cares

for no-one

The Laughing Elephant

stands tall

and crushes all!

No more

Can be done

No more

Can be said

No more

Shall be witnessed

No more

Shall be saved

The Laughing Elephant

Has little voice

But great

Memory

This Creature

Lives in the sun

And lingers in the shadows

You will hear

Him at night

When the moon

Is weary

You will shudder

And hide

For his laughter

Is doomed

For pride!

Laughing

Laughing

Laughing

Laughter

This Creature lingers

In the deserts

of the world

people hear it

laughing

laughing

laughter

filled

with wicked

chime

and

malice painted

in the sand

the color

of blue

and gray

in the

middle of the

storm

This Creature's

        Voice gathers

        Up flame

        And

        Throws it upon us

It waits for no-one

        Cares for no-one

This Creature was

Created by our minds design

The Laughing Elephant is our demise

        Yes, to the light

        Yes, to the water frozen

        In our sockets

        We cannot

        Imagine such treachery

        Lingering in our midst

The Laughing Elephant

Has no face

Nor soul

For it lives

for the stars

this Creature

has little sorrow

and dances

in circles

to abuse you

to abuse you

as you sit

under the stars

and watch them fall

one by one

off the façade

of blue-ish

purple-ish

sky called God's force of tears

He waits

In the meadows

And smiles

At the sun

For there is little light

The Creature

Will laugh

Laugh

Laughter

Will haunt

The stars

And keep

You bent on your knees

With bowed heads

And tears of blood

Who are we to tell?

What is there to become of The Creature?

We stand and listen

To The Creature

Sing in laughter

We hope that it ends

We need

Not

Surrender nor run

The hands

Of man are often

Written in sorrow

The Creature

Is

Far from our lives

It is cunning and lurking

It is real

The Creature is real!

It is alive!

The Laughing Elephant

Is lurking

And hiding in the midst of our dreams

Don't wish to see this Creature

This Creature

Doesn't sing of melodies

Yet the voice of this Creature

Is haunting

And makes your ears bleed

It cares for no-one

Waits for no-one

For no-one

For no-one

For when

The stars fall

The Laughing Elephant

Dances and recites:

"For I wait for no-one

you must never sleep

I watch thee

I watch you

I live amongst the

Graves of those that've perished

Long ago

Your soul

Is trapped in a glass

Cage that breaks

I am the power

The power that crushes your soul

With bits of glass

You will shudder and

Burn at the sound of my laughter

You will live

Learn, live, learn

That you must not

Play with the flames

I cast down from the heavens

I was born from

The ashes

Of the dead sun

From long ago

For I have no soul

I care for no-one

I am fearless

Yet you must fear me

Will thee challenge the sun's burning rays?

You will not

Do you hear me in your dreams?

Yes?

Yes?

Yes?

I am a sun's ray

That lasts forever

And I touch

Every species

Every human soul

I lurk in everyone's nightmares.

I am alive when you close

Your eyes

I live and breathe

When you open

Your eyes and soul to me."

My hands glisten

In the boiling water and I scream

For I have

Seen

The Laughing Elephant and

I realize that my body

Is cold

The Creature's eyes

Peers into mine

And I cannot run I cannot move

I smell the fragrance of the petals

Floating

As my hands burn

The Laughing Elephant

Laughs in mine ear

And says,

"I wait for no-one

care for no-one

for no-one

for no-one

for no-one

I die for no-one."

When the skies begin to darken

              The Creature has fallen asleep

          For he does not sing a song of malice

                    In your ear

Yes, we must,

You must fear

The presence of

The Laughing Elephant

When he does not lurk

                    In the shadows

He has fallen asleep

And you must think it is over

For it isn't

The Laughing Elephant

Lives forever

He doesn't die for anyone

He does not die.

Ever.

He sleeps for a lifetime

And only wakes to destroy

Your dreams and to sing...

A song of trouble

He warns

You that

He is near

And you must wait with

Fear in your breath

You must wait with fear in your eyes

With fear in your heart

The Laughing Elephant is the Creature

Of fire and takes

Form in the heavens

Do you see him?

In the constellations

Of the stars in the heavens?

Do you see him?

For he is there, watching.

For how must one

Combat this Creature?

How can you fight the power of The Laughing

Creature?

One must wonder.

For to fight The Laughing Elephant, you must know

him and trick him.

Though it is painful to do

You must, to survive.

You must not worry for you must be ready

To stand and not wither.

The Laughing Elephant

Is cunning and will

Not fear you.

You must make him fear.

For he, The Laughing Elephant, does not control the

skies, alone.

For you also control the heavens.

The Laughing Elephant is powerful!

Yet you are power!

This Creature will make you endure his wrath with

pleasure!

Don't fear the rain or the

Thunderous clap of the Laughing Elephant's laughter!

Listen and ye will know.

You will know when your time is ripe

To fulfill your destiny.

You are power! I say!

Do you not know?

The Laughing Elephant

Waits for no-one

Cares for no-one

Dies for no-one

Cries for no-one

But he mustn't survive

For The Laughing Elephant must die

For himself.

And who better to make him vanish but you?

For when you control the heavens you send water

And he fire!

One day ye will see the connection

One day ye will die and live again, die, and live again.

With purpose and you will never fear The Laughing

Elephant.

For you will be able to gain power

By staring fate in the eye

Staring at The Laughing Elephant in the eye

And laugh back with insanity in your sound.

When the Creature hears your voice

When he hears your laughter

He will surrender and

The storm will start

For the skies will sing in horror!

And you will control your destiny

And you will control your future.

To kill this Creature, you must

Kill yourself, and rebirth from the ashes

Anew.

For this is the only way

One must destroy this Creature.

How does the Creature truly die, you ask?

It burns to ashes and

Becomes no-more

The flesh crumbling from the darken skies

Of heaven

The Laughing Elephant

Will laugh the last laugh for

He will bring you with him

And you shall rise, again.

Did you ever wonder how The Laughing Elephant was

created?

Why did it ever plague you so?

For I only know how **HE** was birthed.

You gave him his power!

Your mind is deep and dark

With fire blazing!

The Laughing Elephant lives through you!

He haunts you!

For you have created the Creature!

Therefore. You. Are. The. Creature!

The Laughing Elephant is you.

You have given birth to

Something that is most evil

And true

And real

You are The Creature

You are The Laughing Elephant

You are the black one in the heaven's

Night sky

You are worshiped

Yet dismissed

I hope ye lives for truth

Once you've found out it is you

Who have caused your fall,

What is there to be done next?

Will you take the blame?

Is it really your fault?

Now the truth is out

And you must deal with this Creature within you

And I will deal with myself

And my relationship with you, The Creature.

Vous êtes la Créature qui torture. Vous êtes L'Éléphant Riant.

Vous êtes L'Eléphant riant

Vous êtes L'Éléphant riant

L'Éléphant Rire

L'Éléphant Rire

C'est vous

C'est vous

C'est moi

C'est moi

For I am the evil Creature that sits above in the skies

C'est moi

C'est moi

Je suis

Je suis

I am

I am

The Creature that visits you

When darkness falls

And I make the storms bleed

In the heavens while you

Gaze with fear in your eyes

Vous êtes moi

Are both the creature

But it is you who created moi.

For there is no other way

To become un-done

For it's you who

Tortures you who

Tortures me

And this Creature must die

Must end

The Laughing Elephant must end, now.

You must end.

I must end.

"I will live forever in your dreams.

You will need me till the end, for there is no end.

I control the pages of fate

And I will end you.

You speak to me as if to win? Ha!

In a distinguished voice, with a different sound? Ha!

You think your power will win?

Seduce me? Seduce me and keep me alive!

I live for no-one

Care for no-one

Breathe for no-one

Die for no-one."

HELL YEA THAT'S MY GRANDMA!! THE

BADDEST WITH THE LOUDEST LAUGH IN

THE QUIET LIGHT!! IN THE CROWDED

ROOM!! MAKE YOUR HEART GO 'BOOM'!!

NOW TAKE THAT TO CHURCH!!!

On God, you good homie?

You listening to the elephants roaring in

the skies?

They coming for you

They coming for you

At your doorstep

There is blood on your doorstep...

-The Laughing Elephant Pink

The Laughing Elephant Nine's

Book of Spells

"Where there is light you must stand

Where there is darkness, you must find light

Life lives on

Carry on

Carry on

Be grateful for the air you breathe

People make up the Earth's essence

For mankind

Walks in Spirit

You must walk in love

Never lost

Never lost

Never lost

For magic is what keeps us

Alive

For tonight

For tonight

For two nights

The heart smiles bright

And she will no longer suffer

She will no longer suffer

You will no more suffer

No more

No more

No more

There is more love to come

Let it come

Let it come

Let it come

There is more breath to breathe

Never enough

Never enough

Never enough

For the future is in your hands

For life is in your bosom

For the love resides in your laughter."

– The Laughing Elephant Nine

These eyes may deceive thee

This tongue may curse thee

These ears may hear thee

These wounds may heal, one day

My eyes are closed to the wicked sight of thee!

I fear not what you impose!

I fear not what you bring.

My language differs from tongue to tongue

Yours differ from drum to drum

My life shines above the towers

That stands taller than

                                                      Your soul

No, I don't love thee

My hands are too dark

They paint with

The color of the pitch black

Night

My soul resides in the

Black hole

During the time you

Worship your Gods

With the blood you've shed

Yet, you call me evil?

How dare you celebrate

The hands that repeatedly

Choke you?

Your Mothers?

Your Fathers?

No, I'm not matter of fact,

No, I do not dance to

The Devil's music!

Ha!

You deem to betray me?

Forsake me?

Laugh? Laughing? Are you laughing now, sir?

Is your sex determined by grace?

Young man, young woman

How do you feel? When you hear my laughter through

the clouds?

Do you question your Gods?

I fear not what you bring

I keep my voice low

                    With rumbling

                    Malice

For He

          The Laughing Creature

          The Laughing Elephant

Keeps you awake

With wicked chime

He

The Laughing Elephant

Makes your ears bleed

He cares for no-one

Dies for no-one

Not even himself

I know the story, sir!

Oh, you don't think I do?

The Devil you worship

Is true!

Indeed.

Indeed.

You owe a debt

To him

This Devil whom

You have created,

This Devil is

Neither Him nor I! Why lie?!

For man does not understand

Why he lives in hell.

Let me speak, I say

For woman does not understand why

She lives in hell.

I did change

My word is

True

The Devil dwells in the minds

Of these

For they believe that

Death will conquer them,

One day.

For they do not understand.

How is this Creature

we know of

Not the Devil, you ask?

Firstly,

The Devil is mortal

To the human mind

And psyche.

This thing

Does not

Exist,

You fickle

human!

This thing, this Devil

Does not exist!

But, oh, do you exist!

This Devil is the Devil for this Devil lives in your

Nightmare in the daylight

                                        The sun

                                Shining bright

Yet you sleep with your eyes open

Soulless you are

                        Indeed.

I'm surprised that you haven't

Become the Devil

                        Itself.

                                        Do you

                                Not understand

                        That you live in hell?

                At this moment?

Don't hold your hands up

Because the

Bullets never pierced you.

Death won't visit you

On a corner.

She may view you

From above.

She may greet you in your

Sleep

With a smile on your face.

How pleasant that Death

Is patient

How nice.

For you fear her, and the Devil, and

The Laughing Elephant!

Ha!

Oh, you do not know of me?

I am The Laughing Elephant, Nine

I live amongst the

Clouds

But I don't cast

                              Spells upon

                              Your souls

That is pointless

                              You are mistaken

            For you have mistaken

        Me as The Laughing Elephant Himself!

How dare you?

                              No, how dare I?

For you don't know of

                  My tale

Of my

              Legendary plight.

            Have mercy and beware.

This is me, this is I!

The Laughing Elephant Nine

I cursed the ground you

Walk on

I curse the words

You speak

I curse the space you

Seek

I curse you with lethal

Words

With lethal spells

I was made

From the Earth

My mother made love with

Water

And she wished for

Fire

For fire to entice

Her soul

Oh Earth

Oh Mother

I have forsaken her now

And become one

With fire and

Water

Oh, dear Ocean

I must say

I recognize thee

And am in-love

In-love

For I am forged from

Darkness and live

Among you

Yet you, fickle human

Deem to murder

Me!

Yet you are very confused

And lost!

I'm not The Laughing Creature

Nor HE

The Laughing Elephant!

I know that HE must be done

The Laughing Elephant

Must be banished

At once!

For I know how

To do such a

Thing.

Ha!

I have the curse

The spells

Within my trunk

In mine ear

In my belly

In my tail

In my pale

Gray

Skin

That is used for the ancestors

This makes you

Dance

In the corner

To my music

Don't fear…

I say,

Hear my tone

Hear my voice

I fear not what you impose!

I fear not what you bring!

In the name of

Your Gods

I'm lifted

Higher

You will never reach me

In your

Physical form!

Ha!

Though you

Very well

Wish

To.

You cannot speak to me

With your un-pure

Tongue

You must check yourself

Look in the mirror

View your soul

I remember

Every aspect

Of your soul

Your

Being!

You think I don't?

You've mistaken me

You've already forgotten me?

How sad.

For I stand in

The center of the room

My sister

Shares this

Space

With me

In the middle

Is where my spirit

Dances

I witnessed this

World

How black

And dirty

It is

There is no

Laughter to grace

One's ears

How sad.

My sister shares

                    This space

With me

My sister is the truth you seek.

I fear not what you say!

I fear not what you speak!

My presence evokes fear in your

                    Eyes

                    You shake

                    And tremble

                    For I cannot control you

I will not stand alone

I stand with many Laughing Elephants

We dance

                    To our fierce

                    Music

We, Laughing Elephants, never sleep

My sister sings

And I follow in

Chorus

For my voice

Brings power

And guides the fires

Of the hot sun

To wreak havoc

Upon the Earth

For it is needed

For re-birth

I will be in your face

I will never disappear

I will be in your space

Quiet

Yet loud

My laughter rings loud

I order for

There to

Be peace

When my charm reaches

Your ears

You will not

Fear

Nor be scared

For I will sing you to sleep

Kill your heart

With laughter

For I curse the ground

You walk

You must not forget

Me!

For I do exist!

I am rare

I, The Laughing Elephant

Nine

Must live longer

To bring you chills

Make you cold

Make you warm

Give me your soul

Give me your truth

Give me your mind

Your memory I define

I define

My skin is tough

Thick

Because God loves me

For I am God

You worship me

Give me your

Tongue

Give me your life

Give me your words

Give me your vision

Give me your strength

Give me your tongue

Give me your laughter

Give me your spirit

Give me your blood

We chant, we sing, we dance, we smile

We have nothing to lose

We have hearts that beat

From drum to drum

From thunderous skies

Shaking the Earth

From the fierceness of

The ocean

We dance, we chant, we smile, we live

Give me your mind

For it is your demise

Give me your trust

For you must not die

For you have to live

Forever

So that I can prosper

Listen to me as I speak!

I say!

Give me your heart

Give us your ears

Give us your sanity

Give us your sight

Give us your fire

We, The Laughing Elephants, will conquer the world

You must respect us!

We will not be killed nor forgotten

We will not be rotten

                              Off the shores

                              Of East Africa

                              And beyond

We will live

We, The Laughing Elephants,

                              Will sing 'till

                              There is no-more

                              Sound

Why must they kill us?

Why must we die by the thousands?!

For my family starves

And weep as I lay

                              With physical

                              Bodies who no longer

                              Roam

This Land is my home

My sister sings

My funeral song

"Death,

Why are you so cruel?

I fear not what you seek!

I fear not what you bear!

Death,

You are not welcomed here!

I fear not what you say!

I fear not what you pay!"

For you sell my body

For prices untold

How worthless.

How sad.

The ancestors cannot carry me

Cannot carry me

For my body, my physical, is heavy with grief

I have left my mother

Long ago

She wants me near

She wants my voice

To caress

her ears

My Laughter, my Grace, my Chant

Gives life

To those

That pay attention

To what I offer

O Earth

I hear your cry

For the fickle

Human has forgotten about me!

How dare they!

Not witness my presence.

I'm here forever

Remembering my power

Give me your power

Worship I

For I call upon

You to do so

Do,

Do my bidding unto God

For I am God

For I reside with God

In the morning

I shall

Live

In the age

Of the sun

My sister sings

My funeral song

Listen as it lulls you

To sleep

"I want your

Power

I want your soul

I want your freedom

I want your life

I want your hands

For they create life

I want your laughter

I want your heart

I want your smile

I want your soul

I want your body."

I, The Laughing Elephant Nine, will prosper

In the midst of

This dying world

The ancestors understand

My young spirit

But you must know that

I'm old and I honor the ancestors and their wishes

For we must live

Forever more

In the name

Of your God

Amen-Ra

Amen-Ra

Qu'est ca?

Why

Why must

You

Continue

To murder I?

Why must my

Death

Be for sale?

On the black market!

Why

Must my kin witness

My blood spilled

On the front porch

Step

I have sacrificed

My physical

For your spirit

To prevail!

How dare you not remember me?

I will not cry

For you

My Mother has

Drowned in too many

Tears

She cannot swim

I cannot swim

We cannot swim

                    Ever wonder why

                        The ocean

                    Has so much salt?

                    The sharks thrive

                            There

        You, human, cannot drink

                        This l'eau

                        This water

        You need to be cleansed

Indeed.

Indeed.

My Mother's tears

Are filled with salt

For the ages

She has cried

The ancestors know

The ancestors know

My voice must

Be heard

Now

I fear not what you impose!

I fear not what you seek!

I fear not what lies

Beneath your

Soul

As you sleep!

In The Room - 87

Remember my presence in the moonlight sky

It is I!

The Laughing Elephant, Nine!

Ha!

I play no joke on

Your mind

For my laughter is filled with pride!

For my laughter fills your belly with joy

Not malice

Peace is at order

I say!

Ha!

Laugh through the tears

Laugh as the clouds grow dark

Laugh so that the spirits may dance

Keep the kingdom alive

For the ocean of

All shall

Shower you and I

As we laugh, laughing, laughter gives you life

Give me your laughter

For it is vital

Like that of clean water

Give me your God

Give me your Nature

Give me your Land

Give me your America

Give me your people

Give me your water

Give me your l'eau

Give me your life

Give me your child

Give me your bosom

Give me your children

Give me your dignity

For you don't have any

Give me your grace

Give me your power

For I desire

I desire

Give me your Gods & Goddesses

For they are real

Are real

And yet you lie

About them

They reside in your heart

Give me your heart, I say!

Give me

Give me your soul, your Devil, your blood, and your

sacrifice.

The Mother that chooses to

Worship the Moon and

Her cycle

                              Understands that there

                              Is nothing to fear

J'espère

J'espère

                              I hope

                              I hope

You sleep with

Tears

Choked up in your

              Eyes

                              You must listen to

                              The Mother Moon

                              For your Mothers

                              Paid attention

                              To her wealth

                              And grace

              I, The Laughing Elephant, Nine

                        Exist!

                                 And I bare no pressure

                                 To give you my name

                                 Or my laughter

For you have lost

Your hearing

                                      You don't know

                                      Your life sources

You've forgotten about

Your Mothers

You need healing

You need life

                      I, The Laughing Elephant Nine

Listens to the Mothers

And they say…

"What do they say?"

you ask

The Mothers say…

"Why bother listening to them?"

you ask

The Mothers say…

They say…

"Are you listening now?

You look into the

Darkness

Not seeing that

The heavens

Are dark

With the

Tears of the

Gods

Appearing as stars

You are lost

Are you listening now?"

You look to

Find a face

To the voice

It is I, The Laughing Elephant, Nine who speaks to you

Your Mothers

Stand in line

One by one

They give birth

To you

Yet you do not

Trust them

For you come from

Them

Are you listening now?

Is your pride measured

By the presence of The Laughing Creature?

For you are troubled like him.

Are you listening now?

The Mothers say…

"Don't forsake I! For I sing the song of glory and spirit! Don't forsake we! For we dance to the music of the night swaying in time to the Moon's gravity and her force. It is heavy yet she carries us to the shore. We stand waiting to survive. Don't forsake I! We are waiting to swim, to dive into the black and blue oceans of the Mighty. Ase'O! Are you ready to surrender your soul? Are you listening to The Laughing Elephant Nine? He is true! He showers the soul with joy from his belly. For he holds the curses, the spells, and the magic to end that of The Laughing Elephant. Listen to HE The Laughing Elephant Nine! He will not lead you astray. We, the Mothers, stand at the shore waiting to swim.

Waiting to dance in the moonlight. In the dawn of the sun, we laugh. We laugh with lungs that breathe freely. We understand the fiery anger that resides in our belly. We understand that we birthed you through the prosperity of love. You live long. Longer without a smile gracing your temples. How sad. Do you hear us now? Are you listening to us, your Mothers? Why must you fight? Why are you so terribly violent? Why do you teach hate? Don't you know hate is unnatural? Now you must cry with your hands opened grabbing for life and we will not give you any! You will die on your knees! How dare you!? The millions of Mothers stand at the shore waiting for high tide as you kneel. Kneel before us, your Mothers, so that you may live again. For we are the Creator of the spells, the curses, the magic, the witchcraft, the symbols, the potions, of which, he, The Laughing Elephant, Nine holds in his trunk, his tusk. Kneel we say! Kneel and die! Kneel and worship I! Kneel and renew yourself! For you must approach us, your Mothers, in your purist form. You must chant the spells and enchantments of your ancestors in order to worship I! You must cry. When your tears are formed, you will begin to heal your heart. For it will open and receive the spells and the magic and the witchcraft and the sacred blood of former witches, who were never killed. They never disappeared but only in your mind. They come to you in your dreams. They are alive. Are you listening now? Are you looking in the mirror for your reflection? Have you noticed the face you view? That is that of a magical being? Ase' O! Do not sleep. Listen to I and I! Listen.

Listen.

Give us your soul

Give us your life

Give us your mind

Give us your Elephant

Give us your pride

Give us your tongue

For we are your

Mothers the

Chosen ones!

Give us your life

Give us your sight

Give us your magic

Give us your words

Give us your heart

Give us your voice

Give us your coins

Your money

Your earnings

For it has

Enslaved you

And needs to die.

Like you.

Death resides in you!

Oh, evil one!

Give us your eyes

Give us your mouth

Give us your plight

For we will

Destroy you

Night by night

You, with white skin!"

The Mothers never lie

They give strength to I

The Laughing Elephant, Nine

For I listen to their

Footsteps in the night

As we chant in the

Dark sky, for there

Is nothing to fear

My dear, for there

Is nowhere to go

The Mothers hear me

Cry for they know

I do not lie

I Laugh, do you hear me?

Laughing in your ear?

Calling you near?

To worship I?

The Laughing Elephant, Nine?

My sister sings my

Funeral song

It is of loss

And of I being done wrong

For my life

Was taken

Quickly, sharply

Tragically to your eyes

With contempt

You spew

Heartache

Never healing

Put love in your bosom

The lives of the souls

Lost have yet to gain

Truth. I, The Laughing Elephant, Nine

Am able to save thee.

For God resides in my

Belly. This is the place

Of the spells. My trunk houses

The magic. My eyes keep

Life everlasting: you must look

Into thine eyes and prepare

Yourself to view the

Universe. I speak truth

From my tongue. I, The Laughing Elephant, Nine

Will not be ignored.

No more shall I sit

No more shall I be silent

To your tragic nature

Oh, human wretched soul!

You dare to stay alive!

With piercing eyes

Cold and White

Cold and Blue

Cold and Red

Cold and Gray

I will say your soul

Is doomed for pride

Because thee is blind

Thee is blind

I, The Laughing Elephant, Nine

Will dance to your tune

To your music

You wretched human!

I will dance

Never stopping

For your music

Your sound

Justifies reality

And continues

For millennia

For I, The Laughing Elephant, Nine

Will laugh loudly

And dance wildly

Laugh freely, you human

For The Laughing Elephant

Dances for no-one

Cares for no-one

Laughs for no-one

Breathes for no-one

And I, The Laughing Elephant, Nine

Holds the power to

Destroy with the spells

In my belly in my trunk

In my ear

I hear your voices

Cry out for mercy!

Your screams are

Filled with rage

I hear your voice

Your screams

Your cry

Your sorrow

Give me your soul

Give me your grace

Give me your face

Give me your smile

For I, The Laughing Elephant, Nine

Will make you laugh

Laugh

With thunder in your sound

Give me your spirit

Give me your power

Give me your fire

Give me your grace

Give me your face

Give me your smile

And remember I

And remember me

And remember your Mothers

Don't forget them

For their blood is

What you seek

The Mothers say:

"They forget me.

There is a time.

They will remember me.

You throw me away.

I say, contempt.

…Look, you will need me.

I say, the day is here,

The day is here.

I say the day is here…

There is a time

You will pick me up

So, you won't be in

Need[4].

> Mwen di jou a la,
>
> Jou a la o.
>
> Mwen di jou a la,
>
> …O gen joun tan
>
> Ou a ramnase m
>
> Pour ou pa bezwen".[5]

Ase to the night

Ase to the light

Ase to the sound

> Pounding loud

Ase to the blood

---

[4] Migration and Vodou (New World Diasporas), Karen E. Richman, pg. 13-14.

[5] Migration and Vodou (New World Diasporas), Karen E. Richman, pg. 14.

                                        In thine heart

                    Ase to the start

                                        Of every word

                    Ase to the footsteps

                                        Of the Mothers

                    Ase to the now

                    Ase we bow

                    Ase to now

                    Ase to now

                    Ase to now

                    Ase to the truth

                    Ase to the sight

                    Ase to breath

                    Stay alive

                    Alive

                    Ase to memory

Ase'O.

It is time for sleep

To take its space

To take your soul

        For you are weak

        And will be your

           Demise

It is time to sing

My funeral song

O' sister. Put love there.

My life spared by

The magic of music

        For you must remember I

         You must cry

         You must die

            In the wake of the fire

It is time for you

To pray for your soul is new

To keep your soul anew

To keep your mind

                                    For it will not

                              believe what it sees

                              for your mind will

                        lie and never tell the

                                          truth

                                    for its filled

                                 with disease

                                 keeping you ill

                              you illegitimate

                                          child

                           you fickle human!

It is time

For you to spare...O' sister. Put love there.

You must spare

Your growth

And become

Controlled by the ruler

Of your soul

The Laughing Elephant, Black

                                        Lingers in

                                        Your dreams

                                        Warning you

                                        To never cast

                                        a spell upon the

                                        wicked!

                    Why?

                                        You ask?

For who is this being I speak

                    Of?

O, you don't know?

                                        Ha!

The Laughing Elephant, Black

Is the one related

To I and

Shall bring upon

My demise

I, The Laughing Elephant, Nine

Is one who

Is doomed for pride

For my power lies

In your bosom

O human!

Yet my sister sings

My funeral song:

"Ase to those

that listen deeply

clearly.

Ase to the Mothers

that dance upon

                                            his grave

                                    giving him life

                                    giving him life

            for I sing my brother's funeral

                                                        song

                Ase to those who listen

                        Deeply

                        Truthfully

                        Willfully

He, The Laughing Elephant, Nine

                Created his demise

                His voice has led

                You astray

                                    But you must

                                    Stay focused

                                    And true

For truth and Laughter

Is what keeps him alive

For eternity

The Mothers speak to him

And you must listen

You must hear

You must know

For his sound is different

Yet old

The ancestors understand his magic

Don't you know?

For his body lays in decay

Yet tears never fall

Never fall

Never appear

Don't you remember?

The Laughing Elephant, Nine

Keeps his word

For his memory is

Vivid

Vivid with vivid

Memory of death

Dancing in circles

Around his body

As he struggles

To stay alive!

Alive!"

I, The Laughing Elephant, Nine

will not

rot

for my brother

prays for my

survival

yet he owes, I

an apology!

my laughter

has been snuffed

by this world!

What a tragic scene

Blood stains

The sidewalk

Stain the steps

The trees!

My sister sings my funeral song:

"They will remember me in

the House.

Look, they are searching for…

Look, they can't even see…

You look for…in that

House.

Look, you can't see…

When…was together

With them.

Look they didn't know…name.

When…truly turns…back on them

You will know…name, brother.

… Look, the day is here[6].

Yap sonje m nan Kay la.

Gade, yap chache mwen.

Gade, yo pap sa we mwen.

Nap chache m nan Kay sa.

Gade nou pap sa we mwen.

Le m te ansanm awek yo

Gade, yo pa konmen non mwen.

Kou m vire do m ba yo vre

Ou a konmen ki jan m rele, fre.

Mwen nan peyi a,

---

[6] Migration and Vodou (New World Diasporas), Karen E. Richman, pg. 12-13.

Gade jou a la o[7].

We must listen

As he dances

As he chants

        To the gods of the Mothers

For we love him

        The Laughing Elephant, Nine

For he will live forever more.

Give us your soul

Give us your face

Give us your smile

Give us your time

Give me your voice

Give me your God

Give me your life."

---

[7] Migration and Vodou (New World Diasporas), Karen E. Richman, pg. 14.

***

For, I The Laughing Elephant, Black

Will take no

Chances

O, you don't know I?

For you don't understand

That you

O human

Have killed

My beloved

The Laughing Elephant, Nine

For now, he must

Live through the

Spirit world

How dare you take him!

For I, The Laughing Elephant, Black

Will not stand silently

As you

Human,

Continue to kill us by

The millions!

For I speak

In the tongues of

My Mother's

My Father's

My sister's

My wives'

My children

My lover's

With breast

Meant for sex

And feeding

My family will not suffer

No more

No more

No more

Je dis!

Mwen di!

I will not sleep

I will not rest

For I, The Laughing Elephant, Black

Will live again!

Ase O! I say Ase O to The Laughing Elephant, Black!

On God, you good homie! You ain't

listening to the elephants laugh

This ain't Disney, Nickelodeon, or Six

Flags

Ha!

On God, on my momma! My white T

ain't got no stains and I wish to restrain from

kicking ass

Oh yea, I believe in guns, sage, and Bible

ways, guns, sage, and Bible ways, funds, wage,

and holy days...

-The Laughing Elephant Pink

The Laughing Elephant Black

"Where there is light you

Must stand

Where there is darkness you

Must find light

Life lives on

Carry on

Carry on

Be grateful for the air you

Breathe

People make up the Earth's

Essence

For mankind

Walks in spirit

You must walk in love

Never lost

Never lost

Never lost

For magic is what keeps us

Alive

For tonight

For tonight

For two nights

The heart smiles bright

And she will no longer

Suffer

she will no longer

suffer

you will no more

suffer

no more

no more

no more

there is more love to

come

let it come

let it come

let it come

there is more breath

to breathe

never enough

never enough

never enough

for the future

is in your hands

for life is in

your

bosom

for the love

resides in your

laughter

with truth

with truth

          for your body

           holds magic

         and your dance

           will keep the

            fire alive

never die

never die

           near and far

        the spell is cast

      with love in the heart

      the magic will last."

    -The Laughing Elephant, Black

The clouds are often blackened

By the night

Yet they are brightened by

The light of the Moon

She understands

That spirits need guidance

The Laughing Elephant, Black

Often stands at the shore

With the Mothers

She stands center row

Centered among the Elders

The Ancestors

For who knows the number of those whom have been?

Continuously drowning in the seas

Wretched with blood

So sad

The Laughing Elephant, Black

Is sustained with magic

In her hands

Her brother The Laughing Elephant, Nine

Lingers on the shoreline

To protect the spirit's passage

To the Gods and the Mothers

For he, The Laughing Elephant, Nine keeps

All and has prevailed through laughter.

The Laughing Elephant

Fears her

With enduring respect

And malice

Such magic one speaks of

Such bloodshed

Such hearts ripped from the chest

The Laughing Elephant, Black

Keeps her magic

Her witchcraft

Her knowledge

Her black magic

Her curses

Her curves

Her laughter

In her bosom

In her hands

In her smile

In her eyes

In the bodies of her lovers

She dances to silent music

Which plays on repeat

To form the hurricanes

The tsunamis

The earthquakes

The thunder

The hail

For she, The Laughing Elephant Black,

Dances with magic in her hips

Her voice is loud

That leaves you transfixed

The Laughing Elephant, Black

Has often confused

The universe

The Laughing Elephant, Black

Has many faces

That has endured with the

Feminine and masculine energies

                                        Ha!

How powerful indeed, you ask?

The Laughing Elephant, Black

Is filled with trickery

And death and life

A blend of blood and wine

Water and fire

Spells form

And come through ink filled

                                Machines

Recorded in memory

Of that of a book

For the dead roam

Searching for this being

                        The beings

The Laughing Elephant, Nine

The Laughing Elephant, Black

For they hold the keys

To the grave

                            You seek

O human

The dead search for

The Black Room

That houses the spells

That keeps them remembered

For now, the ancestors are

Seeking remembrance

Yet

The devil states: "I am in the

          Mood to save

          Lives with my

          Savage nature."

Yet

She states: "I am in the

          Mood to

          Save lives

          With my savage

          Nature."

Yet

The ancestors' say:

"I am in the mood

to save lives

with my savage nature."

Yet

The Laughing Elephant, Nine

Cast the spell from his sister's

Funeral song:

"Whoever walks

the ocean

must cleanse the blood

must cleanse the blood

We, the Mothers of time, the sisters

Of now

Will no longer willingly

Give our love freely

You must cleanse the blood

You must cleanse the blood

The Black woman Mothers the shore

Mothers the unwanted

Mothers the suicide victims

You must cleanse the blood

You must cleanse the blood

Sing to the skies

On the full moon

She listens

Sing to the skies

On the moon hour

She sees you

You must cleanse the blood

You must cleanse the blood

Whoever roams

The Ocean

The seas

The rivers

The lakes

You must cleanse the

Water

You must cleanse the blood

You must cleanse the blood

With the minerals from above

With the salt of the Ocean

and listen to the Mothers,

meet them at the shore

where the oceans meet

Put your fingers in the water

to ease the tears

to ease the pain

it must cleanse the blood

must cleanse the blood

you must cleanse the water

cleanse the blood

with salt from

the Ocean's tide."

The Laughing Elephant

and The Mothers of time

gave birth to ye

O, Laughing Elephant, Black

you must speak

you must speak

speak with the air of power

in your words

with brazen savagery in your

tongue

with anger in your tone

to kill The

Laughing Creature

The Laughing Elephant

keep your brother

The Laughing Elephant, Nine

Alive

in the wake of the flames

from the sun

as we dance in the fire

to listen to

ye

O, Laughing Elephant, Black

come and gives us

your sound

For the trumpet is

blaring loud

Ase to your

mysterious ways

Oh God

O, Laughing Elephant, Black

O, Laughing Elephant, Nine

We dance to conjure you

to abide by your spirits

Ase to the light

Ase to the night

Ase O!

The Laughing Elephant, Black

appears to those who

seek she/him of the divine

feminine.

She speaks:

"I, The Laughing Elephant, Black

was born in the

night sky of the Gods

so worshiped

dearly

yet humans never

learned the shores

of my Mothers

but yet fear me.

Listen to mine brother

my same

For he doesn't fear you

and your bullets.

For I have heard the screams

and have become the Devil

you seek

For I am not afraid of you

I know where my

power lies

with wicked chime

I speak!

Ha!

For you fear my name

Ha!

say it

say it loud

so that I can

smell your

breath!

From the heavens

I hear ye

say it clearly

for what is this magic you

speak of?

That doesn't require my name?

Ha!

How dare ye?

Disrespect

I and the ancestors

For I share

no laughter

with ye

O being of dishonor

to my great

grandfather.

How dare you

forget I?

Ha!

You have been

mistaken.

For I am perfect

in the eyes of

the Gods

and will smite those

who dare

come near

with malice in their

tongue!

For I am not like my

brother

Mon fre

I, The Laughing Elephant, Black

fears no soul

but will

crush the soul of

others.

My father,

The Laughing Elephant,

is crude

and evil

with a wicked

tongue

you have made him the

Devil

you seek!

The Laughing Elephant

shared

laughter

with the Mother

of time

and I became lost

to the Oceans

with little

Laughter in my

throat

in my belly

for it is magic

and is healing.

Yet

my heart is hardened

and burden so

For I and

my sisters

sings my brother's funeral song,

'I am in the mood to save lives with my savage nature.

To rid the Earth of her lies and death.

To make sacred her breath in the universe

for our brothers die daily

with minimal tears yet we

hear their laughter loud, and near

                                              Ase.'"

The Laughing Elephant, Black

speaks of truth

                                        never spoken

to a human ear

For she doesn't fear

the weight

of your heart

Or your childish ways

O human

For you fear rain

yet it brings

you life

The Laughing Elephant, Black

is near

when you call her

she is in the clouds

dancing with the

stars

waiting for the Moon

to show

her face

so that she can baptize

you

and rid you of

thine

misery

you must shower yourself

O human

in the reign of the Gods

in the water of life

and listen to her sing.

For today I bring you a song

It is a song of malice

It is a song of happiness:

"Listen, for the

clouds glide by

Listen, for the wind

is fierce

Listen, for the heavens

thunder

I stand with my hands

glistening in the water

and fire ignites

and my hands burn

Listen, the ancestors are

talking

making communion

for thee

Listen, the ancestors

are watching

waiting

to set

spirits free

Do you hear them?

Dancing along the waves?

in the middle of the

ocean?

Calling to the ancient ones

Calling to the ancient ones

Do you hear them, now?

Listen, and witness the drums

brown and black

with black hands

drumming

the Mothers,

the ancestors,

the Gods

Do you hear them?

Dancing along the waves?

in the middle of the

ocean?

Calling to the

ancient ones

Calling to the

ancient ones

Do you hear

them now?

I stand at the

shore

in the shallow

water

I

glisten,

my

hands red

from

the fire

of the water

she brings forth life

water showers light with

I and the

stars

she brings forth life

And as I bathe

my body and spirit

in the

shallow

waters

of the

Gods

my soul

dances

and I

shine like a

burning spear!

Do you hear them?

Dancing along the waves?

In the middle of the

Ocean?

Calling to the ancient ones

Calling to the ancient ones

Do you hear them now?"

I, The Laughing Elephant, Black

Was born

borne

With an elephant head,

Gracing the universe with lyrics

That entices the mind

Leaving humans

Shameless

For I only speak truth

      Never spoken

            Till this

            Day

I say,

      Beauty doesn't grace

            Me here

For my shoulders are

      Heavy

And at times

      My mind is weak

With lyrical harmonies

      Often sung for

      My brother

      Mother

      And sisters too

I, The Laughing Elephant, Black

Keeps no prisoners

For that is an illusion

You speak of

I keep my body pure

With remedies

From my Mothers' hands

As I burn mine

As I burn mine

Wanting the power

To do harm

To those

Who do not speak

Of me

In their prayers

I understand the human

Is fickle

And weary

But you must

Understand my plight

And not destroy

I

Cause don't you hear

Them calling?

To the ancient ones

To the inconvenient souls

Banished at sea

For thinking that God is

Thee, I, Thee, I…

Let this be a lesson, I teach

You

And you hear every word I speak

And tell the others of

My name

For you are to blame

And you shall dwell in pain

For I, The Laughing Elephant, Black

Have no tears to shed

Has no grace to spare

For the human mind

Is of a weak

Design

With neurons

Making connections

Yet never

Connecting to the source

Of the Most High!

I recite with glory

In my bosom

With lovers dragging

Behind

I keep them near

Wanting to touch

But I be ruthless. With kisses upon my chest with love

brazing through my eyes. It is time.

***

Yes, the time has come

For spirits to dance in the

Sun

And for her, The Laughing Elephant,

Black

To be worshiped

The power she holds is one

With pride

She, The Laughing Elephant, Black

Isn't one

To be denied!

He, The Laughing Elephant, Black

Will keep your heart

Racing with

Sexual desire

Never weary

Of arousal

The Laughing Elephant Black

Has many

Faces

And will destroy

You if you

Do not use

Your eyes

If you do not use

Your ears,

Use them

And you will know

And not endure

And not endure

Yes, this is the time

For children to be born

Of new Mothers and Fathers whose breast

are not

Made for pleasure

But for nurture

Yet these Mothers and Fathers

Are better than

You

O fickle human

And yet you laugh at

Them

And pretend not to

Hear them

As you stare

To the heavens

Waiting for rain to

Come

Yet you fear drowning

Ha!

You fearing

Drowning in the grace

Of the

Gods!

Is a fear that

Is odd

Why are you so weak human?

That you cannot

Deal with the

Gods?

The beings that keep you safe?

Yet you question their

Existence

And deny their memory

Yet you want to live

                                                        Ha!

Do you want to continue

                    To live in magic?

                With Oxygen gracing

                    Your lungs?

Do you realize that

Your breath

Is

Magic?

And who gave that to you?

The Mothers

The Fathers

The Gods

The Oshun

The Vodu

The Goddess

The Divine

The Universe

                    Gave you magic

                                        To live

The Laughing Elephant

The Laughing Elephant, Nine

The Laughing Elephant, Black

                    Created your

                    World

                    Kept it from harm

                    From the Devil you

                    Seek

Yes, it is known of the

Devil you seek

Whom you may never meet

                    The Laughing Elephant, Black

                    May only attack

You

When you grow silent of her

Move

As you recite your prayers

For The Laughing Elephant, Black

Is female

And male

And you must

Always honor

The presence of this

Creature

Honor this being

As she walks

Along the shore

And swim

In the deepest

Ocean

In The Room - 163

You will hear her

Cry

As you listen

You must listen

And recite your

Prayers

In Her name

In His name

The Laughing Elephant, Black

Is here to live, forever.

***

Today I pray for my brother

The Laughing Elephant, Nine

I pray for his return

The Devil has taken him

In such dark shadow

I, The Laughing Elephant, Black

Am his sister and brother in one

I share both souls in my

Physical

The voice I carry in my bosom

Is one of power, of power

And grace

The Devil you seek resides

In you

O evil human!

For you are not my

Blood

Nor the blood of the Mothers

Today, I pray for my brother

Who shares the Blood I share

The Laughing Elephant, Nine speaks

To me

In my prayers

For I whisper to him, I conjure

Him

And he tells me that he was

Taken

So sudden his departure I miss

Him

So

I, The Laughing Elephant, Black

Am growing weary and weak

For my brother does not hold

My

Hand

My soul lingers in the depths

Of the Oceans

Taken care of by the Mothers

I feel weary and weak!

Today I pray in the name

Of me

The Laughing Elephant, Black

As I sit on my throne

Waiting to

Swim with

The Mothers

For they guided me here and

I wait

I wait and listen for my ancestors

Voices

As they sing my brother's

Funeral song…

"…I say, the day is here,

The day is here.

I say the day is here,

The day is here, my brother.

There is a time

You will pick me up

So, you won't be in need[8].

> Mwen di jou a la,
>
> Jou a la o.
>
> Mwen di, jou a la,
>
> Jou a la fre mwen.
>
> O gen youn tan
>
> Ou a ranmose m.
>
> Pou ou pa bezwen[9]."

Can you hear him?

He signs in the shadows

When the sun kisses the sky

---

[8] Migration and Vodou (New World Diasporas), Karen E. Richman, pg. 13.

[9] Migration and Vodou (New World Diasporas), Karen E. Richman, pg. 15.

With a naked

Eye.

Can you feel him?

He walks the earth at 3 am

When the ancestors

Roam

When the ancestors become

Vital

They work

And wait

For you to

Communicate

To communicate

To navigate

Don't you understand that it

Is

Difficult

To stand?

It is evil to stand alone.

It burdens the heart.

We must dance

We must kiss the

Storm.

The day has come. You will need me.

***

The brazen few

stand in front

of The Laughing Elephant, Black

waiting for her to speak

waiting for him to speak.

Yet the few must understand

that they are not alone.

The time has come

for the hearts of the

brave, the brazen, to cling

to each other. Three by three.

The brazen few

must stand and unite

at the shoreline

connecting the world

one footprint at a time

making life permeate

from nation to nation.

The brave few are

world changers

connecting by heartbeat.

The sound pulsates

through their ears

with the sound of

the blood

rushing to their heads.

For they must run

to The Laughing Elephant, Black!

They must sacrifice

They must live again.

■■

Let I present the Devil to you

how meek

the time is now to present the Devil

you seek

you must open your eyes

now is the time to view the Devil

in front of you

The time is now

To dance with the Devil

feel his eyes stare at you

from underneath his hood

The time is now

The Devil will teach you how

to dance to his song

to dance to his sound

The time is now

For you to dance in the middle

of the dark room

of the black ocean

of the 3am sky shining

on the Atlantic

This is the time of the Devil

the three Devils

riding from the heavens

Yes the heavens!

Now is the time

For you to forsake the god you seek

The time is now to dance

              to dance

With the Devil at night

The time is now.

The Devil attaches himself to

The Mothers

with malice in his

intentions

The Devil is not the Devil

you seek

The Devil arrives with malice

in his eyes

You see, there are many Devils

many are my family

And you, O Human

have killed my family!

The Devil lives in malice

for it is his

middle name

The Devil is not

may not

could not

be the Devil

you seek

For the Devil appears in many ways

yet you

O Human

have killed my family!

The Devil, however much malice,

respects the Mothers

The Devil knows

not to do harm

to the Mothers

yet he has malice

and only this in His eyes. He never lies.

The Devil lives in

darkness

The Devil lives in the

deepest part of the Ocean

The Devil lives

in the human mind

from time to time

The time is now

for the witch to rise

This time is sacred and true

the time is now

For the devil will come

forth to frighten

you

For the Devil only has power

beneath your feet

For the Devil

is your defeat

The Devil

                    will eat you like meat

                    with teeth bloody red

                    uncooked unwell

 you will die

O Human

as the witches rise

cast spells

you will die

O criminal

as you drink

the poison

from the Devil's

lips

you will reside in the caves

with he, O evil one.

                              The Devil will offer

                              you supper and you

will eat.

The Devil will
dance with you and
you must move your feet.
The Devil will laugh
loud and you must listen.
You must laugh with
The Devil.
You must laugh as
I respond to The Devil's
magic. The Devil's spells
are cast through his
laughter. I, The Laughing
Elephant Black can protect
you from The Devil's spells.
The Devil will spin a web
around your body. Make you dance

in circles. Make you dizzy.

The Devil appears with

a smile, a smirk, a devilish grin.

The Devil will whisper in your ear.

The Devil lurks in the

bed sheets of the dead.

The Devil will dance

with you in your dreams

in the middle of the day.

The Devil will love your

fear if you decide to

give in to the Devil's

power. Beware of The Devil

for he will conquer.

Let the Mothers speak at once

for it is time.

The Devil speaks,

"It is time for you to

live in the

power you seek

O great Black

Goddess of now.

They bow. They place

their bodies upon

the ground and open

their ears to listen

to you

O great Black Goddess

of now. We bow.

For it is time for you

to walk with grace in

your feet and power in

your toes. With venom

in your tears and

magic in your hands

and eyes. Look in the

mirror at night and

view the magic within

O great goddess of now.

We bow. Today the Moon will

shine in your favor. She will

bow with her, bow

with her beaming light.

The brightness of her glow

makes your waters flow.

The Ocean blows. The Ocean

sings loud. It is time."

***

"I, The Laughing Elephant Black feel so small and

weak. i'm with truth and will. i feel small for the pain

is lethal. i understand that now is the time for

grievance to be paid. for you, o fickle human have killed my source of living. you have killed my brother, my father, and my family. you don't deserve my magic O' fickle Human. you don't deserve to live in my sight. i don't want to see you nor view you. i feel pain. i feel hate. i feel fire burning my skin. burning my eyes. i feel weak. my power is small. my power is disappearing. o mothers i need you for i know that the time is near. the time is now for me to rise. for our kind to rise. to be praised. to be honored. to be worshiped. our kind our gods. we are royalty. how dare i feel weakness? o mothers i, the laughing elephant black need your precious water, your sweet songs to save me. i need your magic. for i have none. i have none. do you hear my wrenched scream o mothers? am i worthy of your grace? for as i lay in my bed clothes and remember the dead and think of the future for my children, i *understand that my breath is final. o mothers, you are*

true and real for my life."

Now is the time for my soul to rise

Now is the time for my being

                to become

                one with the

                Mothers.

Now is the time to rise above the sea

            and take the moon

            capture her within my hands

      at night

            when the sun is hidden

            behind the earth's sky

                            yet she

                        burns bright

      yet she dances

her light brighter

than the other stars

                in her heart

                is where the

                ancestors' dwell

and today

        I will run

        toward the sun

        with the moon in my hand

and like sand

                the moon will disappear

                my dear

                the moon will disappear

Now is the time

        for my soul to

            vanish into the light.

***

O great Laughing Elephant Black

come back

Don't listen to the Mothers at the

shore

Don't follow the sun and her

beaming rays

Don't forsake us!

We are dreadful

in our plight

we regret our

nature

For we are the fickle

mind human

and we need you, need you

we regret our

existence

for it is

not normal

upon this earth

forgive us! forgive us! forgive us!

O great Laughing Elephant Black

your majesty

is heavenly

is righteous

is pure

O great Laughing Elephant Black

we bow

we worship

we honor!

***

I, The Laughing Elephant, Black

will listen

to the Mothers

and to

The Laughing Elephant, White

For he will

speak to you

O fickle human

The Laughing Elephant, White

will save you

from your evil

ways

O fickle

Human

O you don't know him?

For he is not

The Devil you seek

nor

The Laughing Elephant

you speak

with harsh words

For I know of

The Laughing Elephant White

and I assure you

he is your

savior your God

For you must bow down to I and to he,

The Laughing Elephant White!

***

'So let it be done'[10]

I say unto thee

death will not keep

me trapped in

the dirt

---

[10] Midnight Rising: John Brown and the raid that sparked the Civil War by Tony Horwitz. Chapter 11 page 213 'His Despised Poor'.

that I've

been buried under

Blood is alive in my

spirit.

It is time

for me to

rise.

It is time

for you O human

to

bow down

to your God.

For I am

your savior.

I, The Laughing Elephant White.

And I will kill

I will slaughter

I will drink your blood

you will die

if you do not bow.

'So let it be'[11]

it is time

it is now.

I, The Laughing Elephant White

will smite you

with the fire from

my tongue.

The power of my

words will

condemn you to hell.

The time is now.

You have failed The Laughing Elephants

[11] Midnight Rising: John Brown and the raid that sparked the Civil War by Tony Horwitz. Chapter 11 page 213 'His Despised Poor'.

before me

you cry from your

wicked tongue

Oh human

You must serve

The Laughing Elephant

Black

for she is good

and you must

listen to me your

God

For I,

The Laughing Elephant White,

will speak only truth

will hear only truth

will sing praises to

the Most High and

The Mighty

O human

You must rid yourself of

your wickedness

and hear I

The Laughing Elephant White!

It is time.'

Ha!

Imma be a doctor today to save my

people

On God, I'm good homie!

For I'm the reason for the blood on your

doorstep

They coming for you

They coming for you...

-The Laughing Elephant Pink

EPILOGUE

<u>THE GIRL IN THE YELLOW</u>

<u>DRESS</u>

"I sing in

the name of

the Lord

I sing in

the time of the

past

I sing

because freedom is

near I sing because

my voice is weary

The wind

blows my hair and my

dress dances in the

breeze and I sing

I sing

with little sorrow in my

heart

my hands are

coffee color black and

my knees ache from

standing and I sing

I sing as

if to whisper to the

birds to the dead

as they blow in the

wind and

I sing

to all the spirits above

me.

***

I stand in the mirror

and stare

I stand and believe

that my presence is necessary

I stand in yellow

I stand and wait for I am

the lady the girl in the yellow dress

I stand with a smile. my eyes

shinning

I stand waiting for the Lord to

come

I stand and remember my prayer

my song to the spirits

I stand and smell the fire as she

burns the flesh of flowers

I stand in front the mirror

my hands cold my body warm

I stand with grace in my hair

I stand as the fire reaches me

I stand in this house my

grandmother lived my aunt died

inside, it is time for the burn

I stand and am careful

I stand and whisper a curse

upon the place in Chicago

I stand with grace in my

hair...my ponytail tight my

face still...eyes shining with the

moon

I stand and hear the ancestors

sing underneath my feet."

***

"I stand in the mirror

with folded paper in hand

I know I must recite

the spell

again, and again, and again

'Moi, c'est femme

En le j'aime robe

Danse avec les

Ancêtres et nuit,

Et nuit

Ils sont blues

Ils sont blues

Le feu

Laisser le feu danse

Laisser le feu danse

Dans tes yeux

Dans tes yeux

Et nuit

Et nuit.'

I stand in the mirror

and count to 3

and the wind blows

a breeze through

the bathroom window,

smell of lavender

I shiver

and my dress dances

yet is still

and I stand.

***

I am 15 years old

and am told to never cry

'Because it'll taint my

skin' my mama cried

she tried hard to

keep her tears locked

behind her soul.

I am 15 years old

and I find my mother

my mama on her

knees, head bent low

tears fall

like lava

burning her skin

tainted skin

I am 15 years old

wishing I didn't

have her skin

dark, black

brown, pale

yellow, raped by him

because I wore the yellow

dress

I and my mother stand

hand in hand

I am 25 years old

still wearing my mama's dress

letting the wind blow

letting the tears flow

never worrying about my skin

dancing within the rain.

***

I sit in the living room

on the couch my grandmother sat

in the dark

I hear her screams

she has passed now

before my eyes saw flesh

she has passed

I sit

hearing my great-grandmother's

scream

loud in the shadows

of the living room

I wear the yellow dress

from graduation

it was handed to me

from her

her value lives in this dress

her spirit fits it well

I sit on this couch

being the light that soothes her

yet I still hear her

scream

'Call on God

He'll send you home

Call on Jesus He'll

set you free

For the Devil has

His hold on me!'

I sit and hear her sing

for she wants to be free

free from her screams.

***

I sit in the parlor room

facing the enchanted mirror of

thieves

I appear transfixed with weary

eyes, alive I feel

my brown skin glistens in the cold

light

I focus and I wait for my

sisters to arrive

through the mirror that is

there are five chairs I placed

for them

I focus and I wait and

try to remember the spell

'Moi c'est femme

En la jeune robe

Danse avec les ancêtres

Et nuit, et nuit, et nuit,

Ils sont blues

Ils sont blues

Le feu

Lasser le feu danse

Lasser le feu danse

Dans tes yeux

Dans tes yeux

Et nuit

Et nuit.'

The mirror shakes shatter

and what appears in its place

a dark hollow hole.

***

I am 50 years old

lying in bed.

I can hear my great-grandmother

the slave

screams.

she tells me my time is now.

I accept and understand that

I must leave this place.

I close my eyes

I feel my body float

above the floor.

the room smells of apple wood

and burnt flesh

my body feels old

as if I've seen

1,000 moons

my heart races

like a cheetah in

heat

yet I don't open my eyes

I float with grace in

my finger tips

I feel fire on my feet

it seems the heat

is rising

like my spirit soon

                    I will be gone

          I will be with the ancestors

                    but the screams

                    O the screams!

                                        ***

I will not sleep tonite

the moon is dead tonite

in my eyes

no light

I dance in the meadow

my dress gleaming yellow

A mirror appears

and I stop.

My blood runs cold

for I know what

this means

it is time

for our spells

to be cast

For our dead

to rise

and dance

Four weapons

of spirit

magic

and darkness

to prevail

For my people

to rise

from the

earth

one by one

I understand

and so, I am ready

for the mirror to speak.

***

I stand

in a yellow dress

in the cotton fields of Mississippi

in the tobacco fields of Connecticut

I stand

with many across the land

I stand

and smell the fire

I stand and worship the ancestors

I stand

in the midst of knowing

that witches are coming

witchcraft is in

my blood

as a girl in yellow

that burns the core

of the earth

I stand and wait

for the church bell to

ring at midnight

and my grandmother sings

at 3 am she tells me

'Don't worry,

I will guide you.'

my grandmother tells me

'I will pray for you

know that when

Jesus don't work

this does.'

and with that I say, Thank you.

***

I stand

with gun in hand

my eyes are blazing

The wind is hollow

The spirits sing

They telling me to take souls

to kill

to protect

the time is here

for many to walk

on water

and become the Jesus

we've always been

with guns in hand

we be too militant

for the weak ones

wearing white symbolizing

power

death

spirit

as we cast

the Devil back to hell

with the spell

'Moi c'est femme en le jeune

Robe danse avec les ancêtres

Et nuit, et nuit, et nuit,

Ils sont blues, ils sont blues

Le jeu lasser le jeu danse, lasser le jeu

Danse dans tes yeux

Dans tes yeux et nuit, et nuit.'

Bibliography

1. Migration and Vodou (New World Diasporas). Karen E. Richman. 2005.

2. New King James Version Bible. Book of Revelations Chapter 3 verses 20.

3. Midnight Rising: John Brown and the raid that sparked the Civil War by Tony Horwitz. Chapter 11 page 213 'His Despised Poor'.

4. Blackbird 4pm. Brett A. Maddux. Poem 'america, 12am' page 8 lines 1-25.

5. Contributed by: *Blackpast www.blackpast.org* , 'Malcolm X's Speech at the founding rally of the organization of Afro-American unity', October 15th 2007.